The Story of Sacagawea

Virgil Franklin

The Rosen Publishing Group's

READING ROOM
Collection™

New York

Published in 2002 by The Rosen Publishing Group, Inc.
29 East 21st Street, New York, NY 10010

First Library Edition 2002

Book Design: Ron A. Churley

Photo Credits: Cover, pp. 1, 4, 7, 8, 13, 15, 17, 19, 21 © Bettmann/Corbis; pp. 10, 11 © Archive Photos.

Library of Congress Cataloging-in-Publication Data

Franklin, Virgil, 1970-
  The story of Sacagawea / Virgil Franklin.
      p. cm. — (The Rosen Publishing Group's reading room collection)
Summary: Introduces the life of Shoshoni Sacagawea, from early childhood
through her days guiding the Lewis and Clark Expedition through the
American wilderness, and speculates on her life after that adventure.
  ISBN 0-8239-3725-9 (lib. bdg.)
  1. Sacagawea, 1786-1884—Juvenile literature. 2. Shoshoni
women--Biography—Juvenile literature. 3. Lewis and Clark Expedition
(1804-1806)—Juvenile literature. [1. Sacagawea, 1786-1884. 2. Shoshoni
Indians—Biography. 3. Indians of North America—Biography. 4.
Women—Biography. 5. Lewis and Clark Expedition (1804-1806)] I. Title.
II. Series.
  F592.7.S123 F7 2001
  978.004'9745'0092--dc21

                                    2001006837

Manufactured in the United States of America

For More Information
IMA Hero: Sacagawea HH
http://www.imahero.com/herohistory/sacagawea_herohistory.htm

Contents

Life with the Shoshone

Sacagawea (sak-uh-juh-WAY-uh) was born around 1788. She was a member of the Western Shoshone (shuh-SHOW-nee) tribe of American Indians. The Western Shoshone lived in what are now the states of Idaho, Utah, and Nevada, near the Rocky Mountains. There are many stories about Sacagawea's life. One of them says that the Hidatsa (hih-DAHT-sah) Indians took her away from her home when she was twelve.

Sacagawea lived with the Shoshone tribe until she was twelve years old.

The Hidatsa Village

The Hidatsa Indians brought Sacagawea to their villages in what is now North Dakota. About three years later, they sold Sacagawea to a French-Canadian fur trapper, Toussaint Charbonneau (too-SAHNT shar-bon-OH). Charbonneau had lived and worked among the Native American Indians for many years.

Like Toussaint Charbonneau, many settlers in the western part of North America learned to trade and sell animal skins from the Native Americans.

Sacagawea's Marriage

Charbonneau married Sacagawea a short time later. She did not have an easy life with Charbonneau. When he became angry, he often yelled at her and hit her. Sacagawea did not believe she could leave him. In 1805, at the age of seventeen, she gave birth to a son. His name was Jean Baptiste.

Sacagawea and her family lived with the Hidatsa Indians in a village that may have looked like this.

Lewis and Clark

In 1804, two **explorers**, Meriwether Lewis and William Clark, arrived near the Hidatsa villages and built Fort Mandan. They had been sent by President Thomas Jefferson to explore the northwestern part of the United States and find a direct **route** to the Pacific Ocean.

Meriwether Lewis

President Jefferson asked Meriwether Lewis to explore the northwestern part of North America.

10

Lewis and Clark needed **guides** who knew the land and could speak different Native American languages.

William Clark

They asked Sacagawea and Charbonneau to be their guides.

William Clark, a friend and explorer, joined Meriwether Lewis on the trip to the Northwest.

Sacagawea's Journey

The thirty-three people in Lewis and Clark's group set out to explore the Northwest in April 1805. Sacagawea carried Jean Baptiste on her back as she led the group through the Rocky Mountains. She prepared food from roots, seeds, and berries she found. Sacagawea spoke to the American Indians they met in their own languages and made friends with them. They gave her supplies and horses.

Sacagawea led Lewis and Clark on the difficult journey across the Rocky Mountains.

Sacagawea's Bravery

Lewis and Clark often wrote about Sacagawea's strength and bravery during hard times. On May 14, 1805, a boat Sacagawea had been riding in was struck by high winds and almost overturned. She calmly saved important journals, **medicine**, and valuable supplies that belonged to Lewis and Clark from falling into the water. Later in the trip, Sacagawea saved herself and her baby from drowning in a flash flood.

Sacagawea had to deal with many hard times on the long journey.

Meeting Family

After four months of traveling, the group met some Shoshone Indians. Sacagawea learned that her brother had become the chief of the tribe. He helped her to get horses so the group could continue their **journey**. Sacagawea made the hard choice to leave her family and go with the explorers. The group reached the Pacific Ocean in November 1805.

Family is important to many Native American Indians. Sacagawea visited her family during her journey but did not stay with them.

What Happened to Sacagawea?

There are many different stories about Sacagawea's life after the trip with Lewis and Clark ended. We know she returned to Fort Mandan on August 14, 1806. We also know she gave birth to a baby girl, Lisette, in 1810. Records show that William Clark adopted Lisette and Jean Baptiste in 1813. No one knows for sure what happened to Sacagawea. Some people believe she became sick and died at the age of twenty-five.

Sacagawea played an important role in American history. This statue of her is in Portland, Oregon.

Shoshone History

The Shoshone believe that Sacagawea married again, changed her name, and had many more children. According to the Shoshone, she lived to be ninety-six years old and died in 1884. Many Shoshone believed that this woman was Sacagawea because she spoke French and knew a lot about the Lewis and Clark trip.

Many people believe that Sacagawea, using a different name, tried to help the Shoshone keep their land safe from settlers.

Always Remembered

Sacagawea's knowledge of the land and Indian languages helped make it possible for Lewis and Clark to find their way through the Northwest **Territory**. There are twenty-three **monuments** built in her honor. In the year 2000, a special coin was created in her memory. Sacagawea played an important part in the history of the United States.

Glossary

explorer   A person who travels to new lands to find new things.

guide   Someone who is hired to lead other people somewhere.

journey   A trip from one place to another.

medicine   Something used to make a sick person well.

monument   Something set up to honor a person or an event.

route   A way that you choose to get somewhere.

territory   A piece of land. Lewis and Clark explored the territory in the northwestern part of North America.

Index